Issues In Journalism

MACLYN
McCLARY

ISSUES IN
JOURNALISM
A DISCUSSION GUIDE FOR
NEWS MEDIA ETHICS

2005

Issues In Journalism

TABLE OF CONTENTS

ACKNOWLEDGEMENTS

Two HSU faculty colleagues, Dr. Carolyn Mueller, the Library, and Dr. Valerie Budig-Markin, World Languages and Cultures, were generous with encouragement and advice but I am responsible for any errors, etc.—MM

To Chambie

INTRODUCTION

This little volume grew out of the author's need, in his classes, for a way to stimulate discussion of specific, timely issues that a reporter might expect to encounter. Each chapter raises one or more issues and presents arguments that have occurred or might occur about newsroom problems and policies. Because the primary goal of the guide is to stimulate discussion, the questions at the end of the chapter are integral to it. The focus is on rather narrow issues in an area of considerable importance to today's society: the role and responsibility of the mass media to report the news. Larger issues of the media's effect and its sociological role, and the like, are briefly raised, and it is hoped that this guide also will help readers who will be using the mass media as consumers to be more intelligent media critics.

Students should note that issues of law and ethics often overlap--the stress in this guide is on the latter--and students should give some thought to the difference between legal and ethical questions. The guide presupposes reading, lecture and discussion which bears on the issues raised. (Suggested readings and an index of issues raised are included.) The guide presents conversations between three newspaper reporters but many issues are also applicable to broadcast news. Students and teachers may suggest further questions and arguments.

The three reporters, who gather after work in a nearby coffee house to discuss the day's events, work for the Evening Star, a 40,000 circulation daily in a small city. It is the only newspaper in town but there is a morning daily published in a larger city 100 miles away and it circulates in the Evening Star's area. There are also two local TV stations and three radio stations. The three reporters are Burt, Charlene, and Mark. <u>Burt</u> is a man a man in his 50s, who went into newspaper work straight out of high school as a Jack of-all-trades in both the editorial office and the print shop of a small weekly. He has worked on a number of newspapers in cities large and small. <u>Charlene</u>, 24 years old, has a B.A. in English from a liberal arts college. She took all the few journalism courses available and was editor of her campus newspaper. <u>Mark</u>, 30, is a graduate of a major midwestern journalism school who still takes night courses from university extension. All three are general assignment reporters though they have some regular beats, and Burt handles the business page part-time. Charlene does mostly breaking stories. They represent three different points of view. The journalists are fictional and the conversations hypothetical. The student may sometimes disagree with all three reporters and question statements they make as "fact."

CHAPTER I
THE REPORTER AS ACTIVIST

I t's not enough to just print the facts—you've got to help the reader reach the right conclusions," said Charlene, pounding the table. She was responding to a criticism that her page one story on an anti-war demonstration in tonight's paper was loaded with her opinions. Burt, 30 years her senior, had charged that even by-lined articles provided no license for opinion.

"Objectivity, that's the thing. The newspaper has to be the one place where people can get the simple, plain, unadorned facts without having somebody grind an axe," Burt said. "Just give 'em the facts, like the guy on Dragnet used to say."

"That's what I was saying," Charlene retorted, "and just reporting that there was a demonstration isn't just the facts. You want to show how badly the Iraqis have been treated, you want to do something to change society—journalists have been doing that since there were journalists—it's your duty."

"Your duty," Burt said, "is to print the truth as it happened, Some people agree with the demonstrations and some don't and you have no special privilege to tell the readers what's right or wrong."

Seeing that the argument was beginning to generate a lot of heat, Mark sought to calm tempers by leaning back in his chair and saying, "Now, just cool it. You're both right in a way, but there's a third answer and it's called interpretive reporting and it really means that you give the facts but provide background that the reader needs to understand the facts.

"Maybe the real test isn't so much objectivity, or accuracy, or speed, but fairness, balance, and completeness, though we can't print everything about a story and speed and accuracy are vital. We have to be selective," Mark said.

"Journalists used to think that just reporting what happened was enough. But some stories are too complex, they need backgrounding and in-depth reporting; you know, more like the newsmagazines do," Mark explained. "We used to print serious charges just because somebody made the charges, though we'd usually try to give the accused a chance to reply. Now we see that we ought to look at the truth of the charges,"

Burt continued to hold out for just printing the charges and the answers. Mark replied, "Sometimes, that hasn't been enough."

Charlene wasn't fully satisfied either. "You have to be an advocate to get anything accomplished in this society. Why, if I didn't think I would be fired for it, I'd have worn a button and an arm band when I covered that demonstration. And nobody's going to tell me that just because I'm a journalist, I can't be active in all the activist groups I want to be on my own time."

"Hold on," yelled Burt, "you've got to be independent—that's the mark of a pro. If you join some groups it can't help but color your reporting and, worse, even if it didn't, people will think it did."

"Oh, you don't want to change anything, you just want the whole rotten system to go on without doing anything but reporting the bare bones of what happened," Charlene said. "You've got to go beyond that. Look at the muckrakers—they were activist reporters—and how about some of the editors in revolutionary times in America?"

Mark interrupted to say that the wire services, for so long committed to objectivity, no longer did just the bare bones things. "With TV and the Internet the best way newspapers can compete is to give interpretation but that doesn't mean sticking your opinion in the news.

"What if my opinion happens to be the truth?" countered Charlene. "And not only that—look at the best columnists—they put a lot of themselves in their writing."

"But they were reporters first and good experienced reporters at that," answered Burt.

"The next thing you'll be telling me," he added slowly, "is that the reporters ought to run the newspaper."

Charlene didn't do that then but changed the subject so the trio could relax. The next night she said that the reporters ought to run the newspaper. (See chapter 2.)

Questions for discussion

1. Basically, what three main viewpoints concerning handling the news were represented in the discussion?

2. Should reporters be allowed to wear buttons and armbands to cover demonstrations? What is the effect of this on the demonstration if the buttons seem to take sides concerning the issue? On those opposed to the demonstration? On those seeing the reporter in action?

3. Should reporters join clubs or other organizations on their own time? What are the benefits of this? What are the dangers?

4. Which of the three basic viewpoints does your college paper follow in covering the news? Your community paper? An alternate paper?

5. What is muckraking? Do we still have muckrakers?

CHAPTER II
REPORTER POWER

I n my media seminar at the university last night, our professor was telling us about a movement in American journalism in the 1960s and '70s called Reporter Power," Mark said. "It would have given reporters much more control over running the paper or station."

" It died out," he added.

"Did you read what they're doing on some newspapers in Europe and Latin America?" asked Charlene

. "They're letting the reporters have some real say in how the newspaper is run," she added. "Now that's what we need here—then we'd have an editorial page that hit the establishment."

"What's so new about employees having something to say about the way the newspaper is run?" countered Burt. "Why, some newspapers have had stock options for years and I remember working on a newspaper once in the Rockies that the employees actually owned. You kids think you just invented everything "

"But," explained Charlene, "these folks overseas don't own stock in the newspaper they just work for it, but they decide editorial policy and other important things sometimes too. Reporter power, you might call it and it's about time to bring the movement back. After all, it's our newspaper."

"Like hell it is," answered Burt, getting red in the face. "Did you put up the dough, do you pay the taxes, do you have to pay if we lose a libel suit?"

"No, but I'm certainly an important part of the paper and I'm sure identified with it. You ought to hear the guff I take from my friends over our editorial policy," Charlene countered.

Mark reentered the conversation after staring thoughtfully into his empty coffee cup. "Charlene, you haven't said how this reporter power business is working overseas, and I hear that in some cases it isn't going as well as a lot of people thought it would.

"Of course," he continued, "traditionally, the publisher, because he is the entrepreneur, decided policy matters and, because he has the responsibility for the paper, he has wide powers. And we know that ultimately he may have a major say in basic policy though on our paper, like many others, a board of editors decides editorial stands.

"It's also a bit hard to see how you can run a newspaper by committee. Though I've got to say that we are identified with the newspaper and maybe it's a good idea—for morale reasons among many others—to give us some say in the operation and policy. And some U.S. newspapers appeared headed for it," Mark added.

"Bring it back," Charlene said, raising a thumb and smiling. "Just try to run a newspaper without reporters. Are you going to let the classified takers cover the cop shop?"

"Well, there's a lot to what you say, Mark," Burt stated. "But we have to remember that we hire out to be reporters, we work for the man in the big office with the panelled walls. He can fire us, but we can quit. And, if we have a real grievance or a dispute, we can go to our union."

"But it's not the same thing," Charlene said. "We have to change things and we're entitled to some considerable say about how our jobs affect us. Hell, if there wasn't any satisfaction in my work, I'd go live on a farm. You old geezers think a job is just a job."

"I'm not a geezer," said Burt laughingly. "And that remark is going to cost you a round of coffees and we aren't going to vote on it. Reporters turning into editors, publishers and business managers, indeed. You kids have already turned the colleges over to the students. I suppose you'll want to turn the funny farms over to the inmates next."

Questions for discussion

1. What matters should be decided by reporters? How much say should they have over the editorial policy of the paper? Over hiring and promotions? Over business management?

2. How would you set up a plan for reporter power? What problems do you see that must be solved in setting up such a plan?

3. From your reading and other sources, how well do you think "reporter power" would work.

CHAPTER III
THE JUNKET

If I can talk the boss into it, I'm in for a free trip," said Burt, obviously pleased with himself. "The big company which has a branch here in town is going to fly reporters from several of its branch cities to its corporate headquarters in New York. We're going to get a look at some new research they've done in their labs which might be incorporated in the manufacturing processes at the branch plants.

"Best of all," he added, "I've been invited because I've been covering local business and it's all expenses paid. First class all the way and plenty of time to see the town. Can't see why the old man won't let me go, can you? There will likely be a pretty good story with a local angle in it."

"Well," Mark said, "as on a lot of newspapers, the management has been getting tougher and tougher on these junkets. There has been some criticism of the junkets in the journals lately."

"Yeah," said Charlene, "what if this research is a fiasco and won't be used here. Are you going to say so? How can you expect to keep your perspective when they're wining and dining you and giving you a free ride?"

"Hell," answered Burt, "all self-respecting reporters can keep their honesty and their wits about them. I'm not making any deals and they aren't asking for any—that was made clear in the invite. I'm going to call 'em as I see 'em."

"Besides," he continued. "look at the sports writers, they travel with the team—the guy who used to cover travel when I was working in Chicago went just about all over the world and never picked up a check, and the Lifestyle section editor just got invited to judge a big 'bake-off' in Hollywood of all the crazy places to have a 'bake-off.' It's common practice. And it's no different from having lunch on the Kiwanis when you are there covering a luncheon speaker. Or, taking a free drink from the PR man after a press conference—though I know the publisher does not like that.

"And look at it this way," Burt went on, obviously warming up to his subject. "The paper sure as hell can't pop for that trip to Fun City—so if I don't go, they'll miss a good story."

Charlene replied, "Not necessarily. They can rely on the handouts or the wires, if it's not that big a deal. Though you could probably do more with the local angle."

Mark had a different worry. "It's this whole idea that bothers me and a lot of other people. The reader does not know that you went on the trip for free. You can't be sure that it won't influence your judgment— wait a minute, just relax until I finish—and where does this junketing end. It's bothering a lot of people in and out of the business and some newspapers are paying the reporters' way now. Their attitude is: 'if it's worth going, it's worth paying for.' On the other hand, as you say, it is common practice, saves the newspaper some money, gives you a little vacation, and will likely turn up a good story—though so might a press release from the company."

"You guys are trying to change the rules of this game overnight," said Burt, "and I'm asking the boss for the permission to take the trip tomorrow. And I don't want to see either of you guys ever take a free lunch or a Christmas present from someone on your beat again."

Questions for discussion

1. If you were Burt's Managing Editor, would you let him go? Why or why not?

2. If you were Burt, would you go?

3. What additional arguments for or against the trip can you think of?

4. What about sports writers, travel editors and other specialists accepting trips or expenses?

5. Where do you draw the line in trips and gifts? How about Christmas presents from news sources or public relations people?

CHAPTER IV
THE PR MAN

"What are you looking so steamed up about, Burt?" Charlene asked. "Did the computer foul up your lead story?"

"No, I had a big hassle with a PR man, a flack, a press agent, a space grabber, whatever bad names you can think of. Trouble is," Burt said, "he's an old friend of mine—we used to work for the same paper. And there's no doubt he's doing well, got a title on the door, a carpet on the floor, and he makes good dough.

"But he comes in with this press release. Tells me what a great story it is, wants to look over my shoulder while I read it—that was after he'd read it to me. Asked, me out for lunch and hinted that his client would jerk his advertising if it didn't run at some length. And the hell of it is that it is a good story, well written, local angle, and all I had to do was slap a new lead on it and it made a strong piece for the business page tonight."

Charlene said, "I wouldn't want to go into PR. Have you read some of the critical books about it? An idealistic guy belongs in the news biz."
"Well," Burt said, starting to relax as he poured a refill, "usually this guy is OK, but I think he was under some kind of pressure."

"Trouble is," Mark said after the other two paused, "there are PR men and PR men and we shouldn't. paint, 'em all with the same brush. Just like there are reporters and reporters and we wouldn't want to be judged by the worst. I'd say your friend had a bad day and he sure knows better. But some guys just come or strong and some guys pressure like that because they think it's the only way to get things into the paper."

"Things are better than they used to be," said Burt. "In the old days we saw some pressure and press agentry you wouldn't believe. "I thought one guy was going to bring his traveling circus into the city room. And when I was in Hollywood, those movie PR guys really knew how to put on a show.

"Mark," Burt asked, "don't you think more young guys are going into PR. And they seem better educated, on the whole."

"Yes," Mark said, "I think it's becoming more and more of a profession. The Public Relations Society of America is working hard in that direction. But of course, you don't need a license to be a PR person--though what we've been talking about I guess are really publicists and there's a difference.

'Some PR practitioners ," he explained, " are at the top of the corporate ladder and engage mainly in management and policy making. Some supervise large staffs. Then," he added, "you have amateurs, part-timers, and a range all the way between."

"What the guy was doing today," Burt said, "was what we used to call planting. Hey, have you ever seen how many press releases I throw away every day or come in via e-mail? Some of them on top grade paper, beautifully typed, but with no news or local angle, and some are just disguised advertising."

"The best PR guys," Mark said, "are those who believe in what's called maximum disclosure with minimum delay. The guys who know news and who know how to help reporters even if the news might not be what they want it to be. I remember covering a refinery fire and though it didn't look good for the oil company, the PR guy helped us get our stuff every way he could."

"Over the years," Burt said, "I've had offers to go into PR—as a release writer usually—but I think I'd miss the excitement of the newsroom—on those days when we have some excitement."

"Oh, you'd just miss having coffee with us after work," Charlene said. "Right," said Burt, "because I'd be out at the country club."

"You know, mad as we get at the PR guys," Burt said, "I don't know what we'd do without 'em because I wouldn't have time to get all the stuff they either send in or help with—and I would have missed that story today.

"But don't ever tell anybody that I said that."

Questions for discussion

1. What are the connotations and denotations of the terms used to describe PR people and publicists?

2. Describe several types of PR practices and policies.

3. According to the above conversation, what are the rewards of a PR job? Can you think of others?

4. What evidence can you find that PR is improving and becoming more professional?

5. What attitude do reporters and editors often have toward PR men? Privately? Publicly?

6. What would happen to mass communications news if there were no PR practitioners?

7. Is PR assuming too great a role in news dissemination? What are the dangers of a reporter over-relying on a PR practitioner?

CHAPTER V
AN EDUCATION FOR A PUBLICITY CHAIR

Y ou know, Mark, I'm beginning to change my attitude toward higher education. I'm beginning to think everybody should have to go to college and take journalism. Either that, or spend three days in a newsroom." Burt wasn't smiling when he said that.

"Oh, you're talking about that lady giving the city editor all that guff," Charlene said before Mark could respond.

"She was really hot," said Burt. "Wait 'til I tell you what she wanted. She was publicity chairman for some school organization and they are having a meeting tonight. She wants her handout—which was handwritten on flowery blue paper—to run in tonight's paper, to run on page one, and to run just the way she wrote it. And the trouble is, I've heard that song a thousand times. She said the paper should do it to help the club which had worthy goals and an important membership and also so that her group could win the annual publicity contest. And—get this —when the C.E. turned her down, she threatened to have the whole crowd cancel their subscriptions."

"Wow," said Charlene, "if it had run, she likely would have wanted 12 free copies."

Mark had more to say, noting that her attitude reflected a common public misunderstanding of how news is selected, written, and gotten into the hands of the public. "If she'd thought beyond her own problems for a minute, I'm sure she would have seen that front page news isn't what she had. And that while we might hold everything at deadline for an earth-shaker, we weren't going to do it for a meeting announcement.

"We really haven't done much of a job explaining to people how newspapers work, and I suppose some of the popular stereotypes from movies and TV don't help much either," he added. "Furthermore, people don't seem to realize that if we printed all the news about their pet projects, we wouldn't have any room for important world, state and city news."

"Every now and then," said Burt, "a newspaper I've worked for has run publicity clinics for people like that lady. Usually the women's section people put it on. But there's a constant turnover of publicity people. However, I'll bet a round of espressos that the organization she represents has a national headquarters that puts out a publicity handbook and I've seen several books on publicity at the library."

"Well," said Charlene, declining the bet, "you can't expect everybody to be a reporter—though I'm getting tired of every club in town asking me to be their publicity chairman—for free, of course."

"At least," remarked Burt, "you wouldn't use flowery paper."

Questions for discussion

1. What mistakes did the publicity chair make? What did she fail to understand about news?

2. Have newspapers done an adequate job of telling people how the press works? Have radio and TV news?

CHAPTER VI
THE NEW REPORTER

I hear through the grapevine that the Star has finally moved into the 21st century," Charlene said. "We're going to get a new reporter Monday and he's African-American."

"Black reporters aren't so easy to find, I'm told; I suppose Blacks aren't often encouraged to go into journalism," Mark said.

"Well, this new guy isn't experienced—an English major like me but no journalism courses or school paper stuff. He 's going to be trained here and I think we all should do what we can to help him out," Charlene said.

Burt wanted to know what the new reporter was going to cover. "Is he just going to cover stories from the the Black community? Is he on hand to cover a race riot because no white guy wants to cover one? Or what? Because I can think of some rednecks in this town who aren't going to take kindly to the guy if he covers their stuff."

"That's too damn bad for them," said Charlene. "I think the big crime is that we're only hiring one Black—that's tokenism. Still it's a job for the guy and one is more than zero. But look around the Star staff. Only Blacks we got are working in circulation and the mailroom."

"It's going to be a tough problem for the editors to figure out what beats to have this guy on. Naturally, we think of the Black community but it wouldn't be right to just limit him to that. And I agree with Charlene, if some people don't want him around covering their organizations or offices, they can just go uncovered—he's a reporter and that's what counts." Mark said it with feeling.

"A lot of minority groups are saying they haven't gotten a fair shake from the media, not only in employment, but in the way they've been portrayed," Mark continued. "Too often, they've been rather cruelly stereotyped." "Maybe," Charlene said, "this will help."

"Of course, there have been Black newspapers and a few well-known Black reporters but I don't recall working with many over the years," said

Burt. "Lately," he added, "I've seen more minority journalists on TV news."

"It's just a lousy drop in the bucket," Charlene said. "And the establishment better wake up."

Questions for discussion

1. Have minority groups historically been fairly treated in the mass media? How about currently?

2. Have minorities been encouraged to seek careers in journalism? What is being done now?

3. How would you handle the beat assignments for the new reporter?

4. What has been the role of the African-American press?

5. Who are—historically and currently—some of the top African-American journalists and publishers?

CHAPTER VII
A FRIEND IN NEED

A double for me tonight and a big slice of advice pie," said Charlene almost before the trio had sat down at its "reserved" table. "Man, have I got a problem."

Without pausing , she explained that in the months she'd been covering the school beat, she'd become friendly with an assistant superintendent who was now in hot water over a policy statement he'd made that was found to be illegal. "I found out about it through another source—this guy is likely to get canned though I'm sure he didn't knowingly do wrong.

"Worse," Charlene continued, "he's a kindred spirit, a hell of a nice guy, and we've gotten to be good friends off the job. And he's helped me out time and time again—especially at first."

"And your problem is that he wants you to shut up on the story and say nothing, right?" Burt asked.

"Yeah, that's it."

"I guess it's happened to all. of us at one time or another," Burt said. "We're always cautioned not to get too close to our sources, but what the hell, we're human. I guess the only thing for it is just to write the thing and let the chips fall where they may. Sometimes I think alternating beats` as some newspapers do very regularly is a good idea. At least it might help in cases like this. But it's rough always working a different beat."

"I think you're probably going to have to write it, even though it will be rough on both of you," Mark said. "Try to be as fair to the guy as possible. The story is going to come out one way or the other."

"Even if it gets my friend fired?" asked Charlene.

Mark said, "Look at the alternatives."

<u>Questions for discussion</u>

    1. What are the alternatives?

    2. If you were Charlene, what would you do? Why?

    3. How could the situation be avoided? Or could it have been?

CHAPTER VIII
THE CASE OF THE MISSING HAND

I guess I'm in trouble with the boss, but I still think I did right," Charlene said, looking worried.

"I didn't hear anything, so you can't be in too much trouble so just relax and drink your coffee," Burt said. "What happened anyway?"

"I was assigned to do the follow-up on the body they found yesterday washed up on the rocks in the jetty. Been in the water a long time and it had jammed itself in between the rocks.

"About all I could find out," Charlene continued, "was that they were having no luck in identifying the body, that they had to bring in heavy earth-moving equipment to get the rocks away from the body so they could get it out, and that sightseers were supposed to stay away. They were checking with the Law Enforcement Information Network for missing persons, guys who fell off piers and like that.

"I also found out from a cop, almost in passing, that they had cut the guy's hand off to take to the station to fingerprint it and try to identify him that way. They couldn't get good prints because of the water at the jetty."

"And then what? How does that get you into any trouble?" Burt asked, looking interested.

"Well, I wrote it about the way I just told it," Charlene said. " Started with police are still searching' ... and so forth. I put the bit about the hand in the last graph, wasn't sure t belonged in the story as I think it's going to cause some lost appetites at dinner tables in town tonight."

"The C.E. said that hand was the lead and to rewrite it and really play that angle for all it was worth, also to get more on it. I did, but I still kind of soft pedaled the hand, put it down in the middle of the story. The boss asked me if I couldn't understand directions or if I was too squeamish to be a police reporter. That got to me because I was a bit upset about the hand business

"He finally tossed it to a woman on the copydesk who gave the boss just what he wanted. At least they took my by-line off the piece."

Mark commented that he thought the hand-cutting and finger-printing belonged in the story. "People ought to know how the police identify bodies in cases like this. It's a bit of a gory detail but no worse than many in crime stories. Maybe we really needed a feature on how police identify bodies in cases like this."

"Well, I don't think it belongs in the story," Charlene said. " It's an unnecessary gory detail that the City Editor was playing up just to grab people's worst interests and the story was strong enough without it."

"Hold on there, young lady," said Burt. "That's a hell of a strong angle—it will interest the public; that's one reason they buy papers, for little nuggets like that. Why do you think they watch so much crime on TV and buy those detective magazines? It's human nature. You can't ignore something as naturally interesting and controversial as that,"

"Well, I don't see why we have to cater to the public's baser tastes. We ought to at least keep quiet when we can't do a little uplifting," Charlene said.

"You'll learn," Burt countered.

Questions for discussion

1. If you were Charlene, how would you have handled the situation?

2. What are the arguments in favor of printing the details about the hand. Against them?

3. Is it in the public interest to print this detail? Will it interest the public?

4. What is the difference between the public interest and the public's interest?

CHAPTER IX
THE "BOMB" DROPS

I ought to quit, I'm tired of copping out. If I had any dough saved up, I would, but I just put a new engine in my car." Disappointed and angry, Charlene was in a bad mood..

"Relax and tell Uncle Burt about it. It can't be worth quitting over," said the older man, "Be like a monkey in a tree; don't let go of one branch until you have the next. Don't drop a job until you're signed and sealed for the next. Or if you do quit on a matter of principle, be sure it's worth it. Now what's got you so shook up?"

"It's the damn Business Office Musts, or BOMs, as the City Editor is fond of scrawling up in the corner on news releases. When you're low reporter on the totem pole, you wind up writing most of them and lots of times they're just puffs for the advertisers. I could be writing something significant. If those guys want more space they should buy bigger ads,"

"Well, the way I figure it," Burt said, "is that we hire out for eight hours a day and if they want us writing that stuff, it's their dough, Everybody gets tired of it now and then but if you'd just grit your teeth and knock 'em out, you'd find that you really devote very little of your working time to BOMs

"And," Burt added, "our newspaper is better than many I've worked on. , For one thing, the Managing Editor won't stand for a display ad salesman going directly to a reporter and putting on the pressure. Furthermore, very little space is usually given to BOMs—you ought to see some of the papers I worked on in the old days. One ad and you had to write up their store like they had a corner on the bargains."

"Not only that," Mark said, "but you have to admit that in most BOMs there is some news value. Usually it's a new store, or a remodelling, or a personnel change that seems more suitable for the general news pages than it does for Burt's business page. And you must see a few BOMs and a lot of 'puffery' too, Burt."

"Yeah, I do, but I don't get in a tizzy about it like the younger generation, though I don't celebrate when I see those three little letters. And I'd rather have it clearly identified as a BOM by the editor than have subtle pressure brought or think there's some pressure whether there is or not.

"If they call up and threaten to pull their ads if they don't get coverage, or if they say they'll advertise if we run a story, I just ignore them. And, so far, I've always been backed up. But I could tell you stories about the old days, I remember an ad sales guy telling me once, 'You got to run this, because we bring in the dough to pay your salary,' Hell, if they didn't have a good editorial product working for them, they wouldn't have any readership and they couldn't sell nothing. Besides that, even though ads bring in the bulk of the revenue for the Star, readers buy the newspaper. And they buy it for news."

"I guess it's just part of the business, Charlene, and maybe you're making too big a deal out of it," Mark said.

Questions for discussion

1. Is Charlene making "too big a deal out of it"? Should she quit?

2. What is a BOM? Does it have a place in a newspaper or on broadcast news? How should BOMs be handled? What are the arguments for and against BOMs? What is "puffery"?

3. See if you can find some BOMs in a newspaper or on a broadcast news report.   (Hint: Look at the real estate page to see if you find any there.)

CHAPTER X
THE PRESSURE IS ON

You guys ought to buy the coffee tonight because I am privy to some highly exciting gossip which I am about to share with you on the quiet. Burt looked mighty pleased with himself.

"I'm game," Mark said. "It's been pretty dull lately and I think I owe you one anyway. Tell us."

Lowering his head and his voice, Burt said, "The big food store chain in town has threatened to pull out all its advertising if we don't support that ballot proposition its owner has been pushing. And so far the old man has told them to go to hell. But he's got to be worried. They're about our biggest single advertiser."

"What gall those guys must have," Charlene said. "Anyway, I hope the old boy sticks by his guns."

"I've seen this kind of thing happen before, and it takes some guts to tell 'em to take their business elsewhere. But it isn't like there's strong local newspaper competition." Burt said.

"Don't be too sure," Mark responded, "somebody could start an alternate paper and not only that but look at the possibilities for them to go to radio or TV. Though I believe they're better off in our paper. In fact, my guess is that they need the Star more than the Star needs them. Though we might see a bit of belt-tightening around the shop for a while—now don't get nervous, Charlene, you're not going to get laid off. It will worry the business types, however."

"My experience has been that these things usually are just threats," Burt said, reflecting. "Though I remember a retailer yanking out big ads one time because we ran—this was in the days when I worked for the long-gone Gazette, God rest its soul—the fact that his kid had been arrested on a felony. But he came back."

"What worries me," Charlene said, "is that some newspapers or broadcast stations might not be able to resist that kind of financial pressure. What if they were new, or just making it or not making it? Then what?"

"Then you really have it on the line," Mark said.

Questions for discussion

1. What arguments might be used to justify giving in to the advertiser?

2. Would you give in? What if you were in the situation Charlene describes?

3. Can you find cases where newspapers and broadcasters have stood up to this kind of pressure?

CHAPTER XI
A NEWS STORY HAS ITS EFFECTS

Surveying Charlene's downturned mouth, Burt felt it necessary to ask, "What's got you so down in the dumps? If it's money, I can let you borrow $100 until payday though I can tell you I wouldn't do that for everybody."

"I appreciate it, but what's bugging me is an angry phone call I got from a woman today—tears, hysterics, threats, the whole bit. She blamed me for getting her fired."

"What did you do?," Burt asked. "Is it libel?"

"No nothing like that. I just had her name in a roundup story off the cop beat about drunk drivers. I'd picked her case because she had gone off the road and creamed a powerpole. That's one thing that bothers me. She said lots of drunk drivers don't get reported."

"There's something to that," Burt replied. "Some newspapers list all arrests, usually in six- point type, but we pick and choose depending on who was involved, how bad it was and, I guess, really on how much space we have that day, But she did a bit more than the routine, it sounds like."

Charlene explained that the woman had been dismissed from her job after her boss read the story. He said the notice was embarrassing to his firm, and anyway, he couldn't have drinkers working for him. "She said it was her first offense, she had been to a party and only drank occasionally and it was my fault she can't pay for the groceries or her kid's doctor bill. If it hadn't been in the paper, she said, nothing would have happened. She really got to me. I feel that if I hadn't written the story, I wouldn't have caused all this unhappiness," Charlene said.

"You keep talking that way and you'll drive yourself round the bend," Burt said, "A reporter has to report what happens—you do not make the news. She made the news, you reported it, and if there were any unfortunate effects, that's just the breaks of the game for her."

Mark suggested that Charlene was taking the incident too seriously.

"You are going to have to report lots of things that people don't like because a lot of crime news, especially, is that way. As the saying goes, if she didn't want it in the papers, she shouldn't have let it happen. People who get in trouble with the law may expect to see their names in the paper."

"Besides," Burt said, "does this woman seriously believe that her employer wouldn't have found out about it? It sounds like he was just looking for an excuse to fire her."

By now, Charlene had brightened considerably. "You know, sometimes I think about the general effects of what we do and more often about the effects of mass communication in general. What effect does TV and movie violence have? Can the mass media create a star or indeed change the culture? Can press endorsements get candidates elected?"

"That's a complex subject you have suggested and a lot of research has been done," Mark said. "And the answers are far from clear. If you remind me, I'll loan you some books and journals that have some stuff that deals with the questions you're raising. Right now, we can look at some research, and, like they say in graduate school, more research is needed. This question of the effects of the mass media isn't an easy one. Although from some of the cocktail party conversation I've heard, many of the general public think that it is."

"Anyway, since you're feeling better, Charlene, and don't need a loan, you can buy a round of coffee."

Questions for discussion

1. Was the woman right in blaming Charlene for losing her job?
2. Should all. drunk driving arrests—or none—be run? Should all receive the same space and story play? How should this kind of news be selected?
3. The question of the effects of the mass media is a large and complex one and is only hinted at here because of the narrower scope of this book. However, you will probably be interested to try to answer the questions raised by Charlene and to review some of the recent research and thinking about it.

CHAPTER XII
BAD NEWS

Did you see the letter to the editor tonight claiming that the press puts out too much bad news? I'm getting tired of that old saw."

For openers in that evening's conversation it wasn't as strong as offering to buy the coffee, but Burt got a reaction from Charlene and Mark anyway.

"I read where somebody is syndicating a package of feature material containing nothing but good news and another guy is trying a newspaper that will print nothing but good news," Charlene said.

Burt said he'd bet neither venture would make it. "We used to run a page one box daily of some good news items, not much, just enough to warm hearts and show we were good guys. Now we try to scatter some bright items throughout the paper, mainly to give balance and to entertain."

Mark said people were tired of reading about war, crime and other unhappiness and wanted some relief. "But I agree with you, Charlene, a paper devoted to good news wouldn't and hasn't lasted because people really want to know about the war, about crimes, accidents, disasters, fights, divorces; the normal things, business as usual just does not make news."

"It seems that news by definition is almost always bad news," Charlene said. "Nobody would be very interested in reading how most people safely got to work today, but the guy who stacks up his car is worth some attention," she added.

"I suppose some of this 'bad news' complaint stems from some people's belief that reading about such unfortunate things as crime and war makes people want to do more crime and war—though you can't prove that contention," Mark said. "Just as sure as we started to print only 'smile' stories, you'd find people going off to find out what's really happening. And much as we hear complaints about bad news, I have to believe that most people would rather know about the wars, crimes and unhappiness in the world than have the feeling that it is all secreted behind the scenes."

Questions for discussion

1. Is news usually bad news? What makes news? Why?

2. Would a good news newspaper be a success?

3. Is it right for the press to print what the public is interested in, even if that means the sordid side of life?

CHAPTER XIII
JUVENILES' NAMES

Idon't understand why we used the names of all the high school students in my pot bust story tonight and then the desk edited out all the names of the kids in the malicious mischief story. Hell, it's as bad to bust up a vacant house as it is to smoke pot—worse."

Burt thought Charlene looked needlessly chagrined when the latter said that with some vehemence so he said, "You're just teed off because you had to go back to the cop shop and get all the names."

"No I didn't," said Charlene. "I had them in my notes but I just wrote four 17-year-old boys and two 16-year-old girls in the original draft of the pot bust story. When the desk said they wanted names and addresses, I had them."

"Well, the desk runs the newspaper and the desk runs its affairs the way the M.E. tells them and he does what the publisher suggests, I suppose. Anyway, it's a policy decision at the top and you don't have to get involved except to find out what the policy is," Burt said and shrugged.

"That's what I'm trying to find out—what is the policy?" Charlene responded quickly, "In one crime story we run the names of the arrestees, and in the other we don't and they're all under 18."

Mark said, "I used to be puzzled too, and the fact is there is no policy; it's play it by ear. About all you can do is ask the desk. Sometimes they want juveniles' names and addresses and sometimes they don't,"

"Isn't there a law about using their names?" Charlene asked. "After all, they are going to get different treatment in court than adults, and they can even have their files sealed later on if they wish. Nobody would know about a mistake when a guy was young that way. S e e m s fair; everybody does something crazy when they're young. But with the newspaper on microfilm, it won't do any good to close court files."

"To answer your question, there is a law about whether juveniles' names can be used and in what circumstances in some states,   but not this one. Some newspapers use them always—they believe it is a deterrent to juvenile_crime, Others use them in major cases (like felonies) only. Some use them only if the case involves a motor vehicle—figuring a guy has some adult responsibilities when he gets a driver's license. Some never use juveniles' names in crime stories. And I imagine we're not the only ones who play it by ear. The thing to watch for is to see what happens to the name of the publisher's kid if he ever gets busted," Mark had run out of breath.

Charlene said he thought that the deterrent would be against the parents. "The old man will be embarrassed as hell at work and the old lady won't go to her bridge club meetings for a month. They'd probably want to kill the kid, especially if the story contained the parents' names and addresses.

But they'd be heroes at school—with their peer group as they used to say in my sociology classes."

"Sociology classes or no, I say if a guy is arrested, he gets his name in no matter what. That would stop this play-it-by-ear business," Burt said, "And I don't buy that softsoap stuff about poor kid, one mistake, seal the records and all that tripe. Be tough; that's the way to stop crime. Besides it's fairer that way to everyone and easier for us."

Questions for discussion

1. Should juvenile names and addresses be run in the paper when they are taken into custody by police? In what cases? At what ages?

2. What are the rules in your state about printing juvenile names? What are the rules for court proceedings for juveniles? Are they arrested and processed in the same manner as adults?

3. In addition to the reasons given above, what arguments can you find for running or not running juveniles' names?

CHAPTER XIV
CONFLICT OF INTEREST

You guys should be very proud of me today, my halo is shining; my conscience is clear; I will sleep the sleep of the just; you can hold me up as an example of the responsible, honest reporter, and it just cost me a barrel of bucks." Burt had evidently practiced the speech.

"What did you do, turn down a bribe?" asked Charlene.

"No," Burt said, "that would have been more clear cut. I had a little stock, inherited it years ago, and I never thought much about it until today when I had a story about that company come over the wires. Made me wonder if I could play the story right or whether I might be influenced thinking that favorable play on the business pages might send the stock up in price. But what happened later was worse. A guy I know offered to let me in on a new stock underwriting at a lower price than to the public if I would plug the stock. And he promised more inside info on stocks in the future. Of course, he wasn't with one of the reputable, stock brokerage firms. They call his operation a boiler-room."

"Are you coming to the point; I'd like another espresso sometime tonight," Charlene said.

"O.K., O.K.," Burt said, "I've decided it's wrong for a guy who handles the business page—even part-time like I do—to own any stock at all. It will just make things easier all around. And there goes my chance to get rich quick."

"Don't be too sure. You might hit it big at the racetrack Saturday," Mark said. "On the other hand, you might not. And in any case, I think you are doing the right thing. I think we've all got to be careful with this conflict of interest thing, though most of the attention on conflict has been directed at government officials. You know, some guy who awards contracts to a company he's got a piece of.

"Not only that, but the law may move in on business reporters trying to manipulate stock prices," Mark added.

"But if we cover things we have a stake in, we open ourselves up. I think that's why the management here is so down on moonlighting doing PR and does not encourage us to get involved in local civic organizations and the like. You'll notice almost all the joining is done by the business side people. It may sound corny, but there's something to the idea that a journalist must be independent."

"I think a journalist is a fancy name for a reporter. My, my aren't we classy," said Burt.

"Spoken like a man with a clear conscience," said Mark.

Questions for discussion

1 Should business editors be permitted to own stocks? To get 'inside' information?

2. What other possible conflict-of-interest situations can you see facing a reporter?

3. Must a reporter give up his right to join organizations, moonlight, buy stock, or cover things he is interested in? Can he cover a school where his children are students? Where he is a student? Where he was a student? A law suit in which he is a plaintiff? A city council meeting to raise taxes in the city in which he lives? The police if his brother is a local police officer?

4. If his or her possible conflicts of interest are disclosed, may the reporter then go ahead and cover the situation? When should they be disclosed? How? To whom?

CHAPTER XV
THE FOUR--LETTER WORD

I was the victim of some establishment-type, old fogey, puritan, out-dated copyreader today," announced Charlene in high dudgeon. "No wonder my generation watches TV."

Burt said, "Watch what you are saying about your elders and betters and tell us instead how your deathless prose was butchered. We've all had the feeling now and then that some of our best stuff has been butchered by the desk. In fact, the next war will be between the reporters and the copyreaders, not the Big World Powers as you may have heard." "Unfortunately, the desk wins about 99 arguments out of every 100," Burt added.

Mark said it was annoying to have his story copy edited by someone with no feeling for the story. "On the other hand,. in the darkest recesses of my heart, I know that they have often improved one of my pieces—though I'd never admit it to them."

Anyway, Burt wanted to know what Charlene's specific complaint was. "Well, I covered the protest at the university today and there were several signs and a continuous chant telling the administration to have sexual intercourse, as our copy desk so euphemistically put it. Actually, the protesters were using a common four-letter word," Charlene stated.

"And one that does not appear in family newspapers," Mark observed.

"For sure, just the point, and precisely," said Charlene. "Especially not this newspaper. We're supposed to be reporting what happened. What happened is that they used the word. It has a special meaning, a euphemism doesn't do it, and it's a cop-out because everybody knows what they were saying anyway."

"In addition," Charlene went on really warming to her subject, "that word is coming into the language—has arrived, in fact—and here is the Star, 20 years behind the times as usual, bleeping it—in effect.

"Not only that," she continued, 'the euphemism is worse than the word and you do see the word in many magazines. College newspapers use it, at least we did when I was editor—sometimes you have to use it to get the point across, or, in this case, to report accurately what went on.

"What happened the first time you used it in your college paper?" Mark asked,

"There was a big stink. Some of the alumni, parents, businessmen in the community, even some students, you know, the whole establishment crowd got up in arms. The adviser took a lot of heat. I don't think the administration was very happy, but we weren't about to be censored. The whole thing blew over finally.   It was a few years ago, now.   I think the thing would pass unnoticed today, which is another reason why the Star should have used it."

"Well," Burt said, "I use that word, we all have heard it but it must still bother some people, including the publisher, because we have a firm rule against it. I suppose that seeing it in black-and-white in the newspaper that comes into the home is what bugs some people. Maybe they're worried about kids seeing it."

"The kids have seen it," Charlene said.

Mark said, "Charlene, it does bother some people, fewer and fewer, perhaps, because the language is changing. So my guess is that before too long it will be OK to use that word, " he said. "Society has changed; there's been a great liberation in the area of sex and language, obscenity laws are freer, people's attitudes have changed—look at the movies— though you don't hear the word on TV but that's because of the FCC, I guess."

"And since things have changed," Charlene said, pounding the table and spilling the coffee, "it's a cop-out not to use that word."

"Aw, F---," said Burt.

Questions for discussion

1. Would you have used the word in the Star? In your college newspaper? Under what circumstances?

2. Will it become common for the word to appear in the daily press? On TV and radio?

3. Would the appearance of the word in your hometown newspaper offend you? In an underground newspaper? In a college newspaper? What

percentage of the audience would you think would be offended in each case?

4. Why don't newspapers use the word, and some other four-letter words?

5. If you don't use the word in a news story such as the one described above, how do you get around it? Does the story lose anything? Gain anything? Is the word essential?

6. Should ads for X-rated movies be barred from family newspapers? How about news pictures or descriptions that some people find offensive or obscene? How many people would have to be offended? How would you know they were offended?

7. What is legal obscenity? (See a press law textbook.) Can you come up with a better definition? (Some people say war is obscene.)

CHAPTER XVI
OOPS

Well, I blew one yesterday, maybe I'm in the wrong business," said Charlene, obviously downhearted and dismayed.

"The kid finally made a mistake, Mark," Burt said. "Don't let it worry you, kid; you're human too; we all make 'em. Trouble with being a reporter is that they are so damn public. Trick is to be careful and not make too many. Anyway, are you sure it's really your mistake and some source didn't give you the wrong stuff or the printers mess you up."

"No, I blew it all by myself," Charlene said, shaking her head. "Misquoted a guy because my notes were unclear and it was an important statement at the school board meeting. At first I thought he was like some guys I've run into before.

"You know, they say it, then when it comes out in the paper and they either start getting some heat or realize how dumb they look, they claim they were misquoted. But that guy had a tape of this meeting, and I had him wrong. I think I'm going to start using a tape recorder myself, more and more reporters are," Charlene said.

"Well, then they'll just say you quoted them out of context because you didn't print every word they said or you summarized it. Of course, it's possible to quote out of context, but we can't run everything," Burt said.

"You know, I'm surprised there aren't more mistakes in newspapers when you figure the speed at which we work and the fact that we often have to rely on second-hand information. Just go to the scene of an accident and listen to the witnesses' stories. You'll think they all saw different wrecks," Burt added.

"That's all very interesting but it does not help me. The guy is hollering for a retraction even though we didn't libel him but only misquoted him. What should I do?" Charlene asked.

"When a newspaper makes a mistake, its duty is clear. It should correct it as soon as possible on its own initiative. The American Society of Newspaper Editors Canons of Ethics makes that clear," Mark said. "I'm going to hit you over the head with a copy of the canons if you won't read them on your own. They cover such things as sincerity, truthfulness, accuracy, independence and a number of other important areas. I'd like to see them rigidly adhered to and enforced. It would stop a lot of criticism of the press, and it would stop a lot of talk about increased legal limitations of the news media—laws that would be unconstitutional anyway."

"Some people talk about a right of reply law, though I don't know how they could ever administer one, and I think it's unconstitutional," Burt said. "Hell, we've already got libel laws."

"I think a press council might be one answer for some of the criticisms of the press," Mark said, "though they've never caught on here as they have in Europe. And I'd want to make sure the people on the council knew what they were talking about. And Charlene, try to see your correction gets in our corrections column as soon as possible."

"You mean every time we goof or somebody we rely on does, we have to correct?" Charlene asked.

"Everyday, on page two." Mark said. "If it's not our mistake, we shouldn't take the blame for it though we should correct it. Now relax and stop worrying and have another coffee. It isn't the end of the world, as Burt said; it has happened to all of us."

Questions for discussion

1. What is the difference between a retraction of a libel and correction of the kind of mistake described above?

2. What other ethical issues are discussed in the ASNE Canons of Ethics? How are the canons enforced?

3. What other codes of ethics relate to journalism?

4. Do you agree with Mark about the correction? About press councils?

5. How do press councils work? What recent developments have there been in the U.S. concerning press councils?

6. How do right of reply laws work? What are their pros and cons?

7. Is journalism a profession? A trade? A business? Would greater stress on codes of ethics make it a profession?

8. If you have found other ethics canons from journalism organizations, how does the Society of Professional Journalists statement differ from the others?

CHAPTER XVII
THE SCOOP

Congratulations, kid, I'm buying your espresso tonight. That was quite a story about the shenanigans at City Hall," Burt greeted Charlene.

"Thanks," Charlene replied "it was tough to get, but worth it. Page one by-line, clean beat on everybody else including radio and TV, scooped the whole area. I'm going to ask for a raise."

"That was a good piece of reporting about how the city is going to come up thousands short of the budgeted income this year. It looks like somebody better be worrying about a grand jury indictment tonight," Mark said. "How did you get it?"

"I got a tip from a friend of mine. Then I had to try to chase the thing down and get somebody to talk. I just kept pushing, asking, demanding, yelling until the City Treasurer gave me a carefully-worded statement.

"But that was only the start of it. He wanted to know where I'd found out about it--they're still making noises about suing me to make me reveal my source so they can get him. They may claim he's guilty. I'm not talking," Charlene said. "I know we have a rule that says my editor has to know my source and she does. How about testifying in court?"

"I wouldn't worry too much; this state has a shield law," Mark said, "though a '72 decision of the U.S. Supreme Court makes me afraid legally in case I might be subpoenaed by a grand jury."

"Law or not, I promised the guy secrecy and that's what he's going to get," Charlene said. "It's like a doctor-patient or lawyer-client relationship. We need a shield law that protects against grand juries and a federal shield law as well as a state law."

"Well, not exactly, but I agree with you that you should keep the guy's name secret," Mark said. "What happened next?"

"The city officials tried to say they couldn't give me any more information because it was not public information. They said they'd announce it in due course," Charlene said. "With a little help from the Managing Editor., we convinced them it was public information"

"Then they started putting pressure on the publisher to drop the story because it would embarrass the city, ruin at least one career, and would hurt business in town. He told them to stuff it," Charlene continued.

"Next, they said they'd sue for libel if I printed it, but the M.E. said they didn't have a chance.

"Now that the story is out, they are claiming that I conspired to get secret information, that my story is based on off-the-record material—it isn't, everything I was able to turn up was on the recor d—and that I didn't tell their side of it.

"As for that off-the-record shot," Charlene continued, looking pleased with herself, "some of the material was furnished off the record originally but I was able to chase it all down through other sources before publication.

"And as for the complaint that I didn't tell their side of it, what they mean is that they didn't agree with the story and didn't like it. I called every city official who could be involved in advance, and nobody would talk.

"I just got a bunch of 'no comments.' I'm going around on it again tomorrow, and I'll bet I get some comments," Charlene said.

"Well, that off-the-record stuff is getting to be more of a problem every day," Mark said, changing the subject. "In Washington, they used to have a strict code about off-the-record stuff and background information briefings and how they could be used. Got quite complicated. More recently, many journalists are unhappy with it and have told what was said and by whom."

Burt said that off-the-record information and background information had often been a problem for him."What if you are able to chase it down later for the record like Charlene did?" he asked. "Are you supposed to keep it secret?"

"I know guys who won't accept background or off-the-record information. Causes too many problems. They tell their sources, 'when you talk to me, you talk for the record.' I remember covering a meeting once, some civic reform group, and it got quite hot and heavy. When the meeting ended, the chairman announced it was all off the record.

Like hell, it was, it was a public meeting. That's about as bad as your situation with the officials claiming that government budget stuff is secret, Charlene. Who do those guys think they're working for?" Burt concluded.

"Wait until you hear the rest," Charlene said. "When the city treasurer finally gave me a statement, he said he wanted to check the story over in advance to make sure it was accurate and fair. I told him what he could do with that."

"I have shown stories to sources on occasion, especially if they deal with science or some technical field, but always with the clear understanding of what is being checked—the technical material not the way the story is written," Charlene said. "But this guy didn't want to check it for accuracy; he wanted to edit it."

"Anyway, Charlene," Mark said, "it was a good job."

Questions for discussion (see also Chapter 35)

1. Several questions of ethics and policy are raised in the above. How many can you identify?

2. What is the legal situation in your state and in the federal courts concerning protecting sources? Protecting information? What have the recent developments been?

3. Is Charlene right that the relationship of a journalists to her or his source is the same as a doctor-patient, lawyer-client relationship? Why or why not?

4. Leaving aside the legal question and concentrating on the ethical issue, would you reveal a source, off-the-record information, background material or the source of this? Discuss the difference between revealing sources and revealing information.

5. Under what circumstances would you reveal sources? Off-the-record information?

6. Did Charlene rightly handle each of the ethical questions she faced? Why or why not?

CHAPTER XVIII
WE WANT TO TELL OUR STORY

We were talking about right of reply laws the other night, and again today at lunch you were saying they might be considered as part of an argument over who gets access to the mass media, but I can think of a more serious question of access to the media," Charlene said.

"What's that?" Mark wanted to know.

"I know these people, my age, some of them friends, who have organized a new political party locally. They want to change the drug laws and laws about sexual behavior; they want to start taxing the rich and making the corporations more responsible to consumers. They also want to protect the environment. They get about a graph and a half every time they have a meeting."

"The reason they get short shrift," Burt said, "is because the organization is composed of about 20 wide-eyed kooks who don't have 18 cents between them and no political clout."

"So if you're small, poor, and have no clout, you don't get in the establishment media, huh, is that the way it's supposed to work in a democracy?" Charlene asked, incensed.

"Get down off your high horse," Burt said. "They are just not very newsworthy."

"Their ideas are. They are going to have a demonstration in front of the newspaper office soon, I think, and claim they are being denied a right to present their platform They say the newspaper is like a public utility and has the responsibility to present their views. They want a whole page to start out with and a column every week," Charlene said.

"Why don't they buy an ad? What if every group did that?" Burt asked. "And this isn't radio or TV, you know, no equal time or fairness doctrine for newspapers.

"Besides," Burt continued, "they're free to start their own newspaper, or they can call a meeting and tell their ideas to anyone who wants to come." "Starting a newspaper costs millions," Charlene said.

"Not the alternate kind," Burt said.

"Well, they have one good argument, and that's the monopoly situation here—no competition so that they are stymied if they can't get our paper to cover them."

"No competition!", Burt yelled. "What about TV; what about the papers from the city; what about newsmagazines?"

"It's everybody-cool-it time again, friends," Mark said. "This monopoly talk comes about because there have been a lot of consolidations and mergers, and some failures. Some people don't like the rise of the chains, but newspapers are a business and you can't force a guy to stay in business while he's losing money. The kind of situation I worry about is if there is one newspaper, one TV station, and a radio station in one town, all owned by the same guy. But even then, he could run a responsible operation. And usually there is competition between broadcasters and the newspaper."

Questions for discussion

1. Do you think newspapers and broadcasting shy away from controversial new issues or fail to give adequate coverage to groups like the above?

2. What does the Report of the Commission on Freedom of the Press (Hutchins Commission) say about this point? About related points?

3. Is the newspaper a utility?

4. Should print also be covered by equal time and the fairness doctrine? Why isn't it? What is the difference between equal time and the fairness doctrine?

5. How should the group above be covered by the newspaper?

CHAPTER XIX
A QUESTION OF COVERAGE

I hear that a guy who just graduated from my journalism school got a full-time job as an environmental reporter on a big paper in the midwest. That would be an interesting job," Mark said.

"That's what we ought to have," Charlene said, "instead of having all of us cover it as it comes up on our beats and having one guy write a weekly environmental column."

"Oh, it's just another fad. Everybody's getting on the bandwagon. Have you seen the ads lately?" Burt asked.

"It's not a fad," Charlene replied, "and if newspapers want to be where young readers are, they better stop printing so much stuff about movie stars, trivia, and unimportant stuff and start concentrating on important things like the environment, women's rights, new movements in the arts, and the new politics."

"Well, we've made great strides in line with the Feminist movement," Burt said. "The old society page is a lifestyle page now, with a variety of stories on things like what to buy and how to get a job. Never used to see anything but weddings, engagements, debutante balls and recipes. In fact, maybe we've gone too far; I hear some of the old families and old clubs are complaining they never get covered like they used to. Some brides might want to go back to the old days of big pictures for weddings, too.

"We've got an equal hiring and promotion policy for women and moved a couple of women reporters from features to general assignment," he added. "We may have a female publisher soon ."

"We're still not doing enough," Charlene replied. "We have special sections on bridge, chess, the comics, movies, but not on the kinds of things that are really happening. Not the significant things. And certainly not the new directions in art, music, and politics."

<u>Questions for discussion</u>

1. Is Charlene right? Give evidence to support your view.

2. Does the mass media do an adequate job on the environment, women's liberation, other controversial areas?

3. What area would receive more coverage if you were editor? Less coverage?

4. Why do newspapers have bridge, chess, astrology and similar columns?

5. Would you say newspapers and broadcasters put too much or not enough stress on each of the following areas: sports, women, entertainment, science, education, religion, crime, foreign affairs, politics, local government, young people, minorities?

CHAPTER XX
THE RELEASE DATE

R elease dates are complicating my life," Mark said. "I think I'll have another espresso."

"It probably won't help," Burt said. "What's the matter, did a local service club put a release date on their weekly meeting notice because it says in the publicity books that you're supposed to?"

"Well, that has been a problem, but I've just ignored that kind of stuff. The big problem is a story I have based on a news release from the Regional Planning Commission. The release, on which the story relies heavily, is marked with a 'not for release' until tomorrow at 6 p.m. I've got the story and it's ready to go. If I write it for the first edition, it will be on the streets at noon tomorrow, and we're sure to get some complaints either from the other media or from the commission's PR guy," Mark said.

"But if I write it for the home edition, it will still be in most homes by 5 and I'm still open to complaints," he continued.

"And if I don't write it for tomorrow's paper at all, it will be on the six o'clock news, everybody will see it on TV and when we come out day after tomorrow, we'll be badly scooped and look dumb."

"One time, I wrote a clean beat, gave the story to a wire service and it was on the air on the local radio station before our presses ran. I scooped myself," Burt said.

"Any advice you can give me will be appreciated," Mark concluded.

Questions for discussion

1. Advise Mark. Should he run it in tomorrow's paper? Should he honor the release date no matter what as the honest and proper thing to do and something he would expect of others? Should he kick the decision up to the management? Should he call the commission and try to get an earlier release date? What if the commission says no?

CHAPTER XXI
THE EDITORIAL WRITER

O ne of my old friends, Herman the editorial writer, quit today," Burt said. "We ought to have had him along for coffee. He's quitting in a huff, says he can't write most of the editorials because he no longer agrees with the paper's editorial policy, especially our endorsements for the November election."

"A man of some principle," Charlene said. "I hope he gets a good job someplace else."

"Well, I think an editorial writer hires out to write the positions taken by the paper. He helps out with the political process because even if he does not agree with what he's writing, he contributes to the debate by effectively expressing those ideas," Burt said.

"'You can't make a guy write against his conscience," Charlene said. "The guy should have known our policies before he came here. Besides he isn't—wasn't—the only editorial writer on the paper. An editorial board of management decides the policy but rarely is an editorial checked by the boss before it runs—except his own, of course—and nobody has to write one they don't agree with. They meet and decide who is going to write what. Trouble with Herman was that he was finding fewer and fewer he could write."

"Herman really felt that the newspaper's editorial endorsements and positions were making a big difference," Mark said. "For example, the reason he felt so strongly about the election endorsements was that he felt he might have a hand in giving the election to a candidate he can't stand. But I think he's over-rating the power of the power of the editorial, what with TV, personal contacts and a lot of other things influencing how people vote."

"Most people vote the way their old man did, anyway," Burt said.

"Damned if I do," Charlene replied. "People vote their economic interest. Besides it's the candidate who has the most money and gets the most exposure—especially on TV—who wins."

"You guys are oversimplifying this thing beyond belief," Mark said. "There are many variables influencing voting behavior and there has been recent research on whether endorsements—print or broadcast—influence voting. The question is complicated and not fully resolved, and you guys are just stating slogans.

"But I've got to admit, I don't know whether Herman did the right thing or not."

Questions for discussion

1. Do newspaper and broadcast endorsements decide elections? Cite recent research.

2. Was Herman right?

3. Who should decide editorial policy?

4. Discuss the role of the "op. ed." page in terms of expressing a wider range of views than the traditional editorial page. Would Herman have been happier writing for the "op. ed." page? (Op. ed. means the page opposite the editorial page which is usually reserved for comment, interpretation, guest or different views and columns.)

CHAPTER XXII
THE PICTURE

Good sports photo played big tonight," Burt said. "Showed the star of the community college football game catching a pass in the end zone to win last night's ball game. The ball was just on his fingertips and he was stretching for it. Every now and then one of our photo guys comes up with a winner. Don't tell them I said that."

"I was talking to one of the shooters who went with me on an assignment today." Charlene said. "The player missed that pass. The one he caught to win the game was a similar pass and a similar catch but the photographer was getting a hot dog. So they went to the computer, found a football and added it; I don't know exactly how they do it, but they can do wonderful things with photo programs on the computer.

"At first, I was outraged," she continued. "But the camera guy said that, after all, it was a similar catch; we didn't print anything that wasn't true."

"The ones I worry about are more doctored than that," Mark said. "I've heard of putting two images together to make guys look like they are talking to each other when they weren't, or cropping a photo so a big crowd looks small, or using a lens that makes people look closer than they really were. And eliminating people from the final image—not just a drink in a guy's hand but the whole guy."

Questions for discussion

1. How far can photographers go in "improving" pictures? Where do you draw the line?
2. Does the camera ever lie?

CHAPTER XXIII
THE EVENT

A friend of mine from school was passing through town today. He is really antiwar and he was telling me he got involved in a peace demonstration on the West Coast a while back and a TV news guy told him that if he wanted to get his picture on the news, he should throw a rock at the Federal Building. The news guy said that, after all, the purpose of the demonstration was to get attention.

Charlene shook her head when she made that announcement. It "My friend didn't do it."

Mark said, "I've heard stories like that, but I've never seen it happen."

Burt said, "You know, that demonstrator was creating news and trying to draw attention to his cause, and he did the right thing in refusing to toss the rock, but it seems to me we are giving more and more coverage to created news based on demonstration. It's gone way beyond the old pseudo-events

"You ought to see all the stories I do based on pseudo-events such as ribbon-cuttings for highways, laying cornerstones for buildings, or opening a new store with a big ceremony. Somebody's creating an event mostly to get news coverage. Look at some of the stunts."

"Well, there is some news in those events," Mark said. "I think it is a far different thing to ask somebody who is demonstrating to throw a rock, and I'm not sure the issues are in the same ballpark."

Questions for discussion

1. Comment on each of the above pseudo- events: ribbon cutting, ground breakings, grand openings, demonstrations. (Pseudo-events are events created for media coverage). Can you think of other staged or semi-staged events? Look for "pseudo-events" in your newspapers and in broadcast news reports you hear or watch. Why are these stories used?

2. Comment on the request to throw the rock. What if rocks had been thrown earlier and the TV cameraman had missed it?

CHAPTER XXIV
THE LETTER

Well, I see we have three letters to the editor in the newspaper tonight—all of them very complimentary to the paper," said Charlene, obviously building up to something.

"So what?" said Burt, forcing the issue.

"Well, a guy I know who is mad about our editorials wrote in three letters—really nasty ones rapping the newspapers—and none of them ever got printed. There ought to be a law for newspapers like equal time for broadcasting. Maybe we even need something like the old fairness doctrine that used to apply to broadcasters."

"Newspapers aren't broadcast stations—they don't use the public airways—and there's no law that says you have to print a letter to the editor. Are we going to argue that right of reply business again?" Burt said.

"But look, how does a guy get a critical letter into our paper?" Charlene said. "We only print them sometimes."

"This letters to the editor thing is a real problem," Mark said, breaking into the conversation. "First, we can't print all the letters we get because there are just too many of them. So the editorial page editor tries to pick the ones that are the most representative, or the most controversial."

"Or the most nutty, because if some clown writes in with a scheme to build the new city hall upside down, it will get in for sure because it's funny," Charlene said. "And a letter that's critical is probably headed for the round file."

"There are other reasons we don't use letters. If they're libelous or in bad taste, if they're too long, if they duplicate another recent letter, and our guy is especially strong against mimeographed letters, especially those from out of town," Mark explained.

"There's no law that a newspaper has to print a letter to the editor; that law would be against the First Amendment," Burt said. "Besides, you have to be careful to avoid printing a lot of similar letters just because someone started a letter-writing campaign on a particular issue."

"Well, there's no law saying we can't print letters critical of our newspaper. Besides, a lot of good stuff turns up in letters to the editor. And we ought to have an expanded 'action-line' kind of column where people can write in and get the newspaper to go to bat for them if they've been done in by some government agency or some merchant," Charlene said.

"I think we ought to print anonymous letters too. That way, people who are afraid to criticize the government might speak up," Charlene continued. "That's crazy," Burt said. "It can get you into all kinds of legal trouble. Besides, if a guy believes in what he's saying, he ought to have the guts to sign his name."

Mark said, "Yeah, but we'll withhold the signature from the newspaper if the writer requests it, and we can see printing his name might embarrass him."

"We don't sign our editorials," countered Charlene.

"That's because they are the view of the newspaper as an institution and newspapers have been taking stands for decades—maybe centuries," Mark said. "The editorial isn't the opinion of one guy—it's the opinion of the newspaper."

Charlene said, "I can't shake the feeling that the reason we print so many complimentary letters and few critical ones is that the Managing Editor thinks it impresses the publisher that the editorial department is doing a great job. He's got some formula that each letter represents 50 people who didn't write."

"That's terribly unscientific," Mark said. "Letters to the editor are no public opinion poll. I think that the people who write are often the people at the extremes of an issue and people who feel very strongly about an issue. It takes a lot of time to write a letter. You don't see too many moderate letters. And trying to judge whether the public likes our paper on the basis of letters is pretty shaky."

Burt asked, "But how do you know if the newspaper is pleasing the public except through letters to the editor and the circulation figures? If circulation is rising, we must be doing something right."

"How do you know what is making circulation go up?" Mark said. "The last time it went up, the managing editor said it was because of great reporters, the shop foreman said it was improved printing, the feature editor said it was the new comics, and the circulation department said it was because of a new drive to get people to subscribe. The carriers get a bonus if they bring in a bunch of subscriptions so they've been hustling for new customers."

"Letters might be a good way to judge if people liked comics, or columns, or other features," Charlene said. "You could drop a comic or a column and see if anybody wrote in to complain."

"Yes, that's one way, but a better way would be a readership survey," Mark said. "And they cost a lot of money."

"We've ranged pretty far afield in this conversation," Charlene said. "However, my basic question still stands: if a guy writes a letter to the editor criticizing the newspaper's editorial position, and it isn't published, how can he get his views in print?"

Questions for discussion

1. What is the answer to Charlene's last question?

2. How would you select letters to the editor? What letters would you leave out? Why?

3. How many letters does your local newspaper print? Do they have a stated policy appearing in the newspaper about requirements (signatures, length, etc.) for letters?

4. Should letters to the editor be signed? Should the writer's name be withheld by the newspaper on request?

5. How does a newspaper, magazine or broadcast station know how well it is doing in the eyes of the public? Can it rely on letters to the editor or some other form of "feedback"?

6. What is "feedback" in mass communication?

7. How should comics, columns and other features be selected?

CHAPTER XXV
THE SKYJACKING

What was the big argument on the copy desk today, Burt?" Charlene wanted to know.

"There's some feeling, and I think the publisher agrees, that when we go big with a skyjacking story, especially when there has been a rash of them, we encourage skyjacking. The argument was over how to play the story," Burt said.

Mark said, "I think the big problem is when the media publish all the details of how the skyjacker went about it. But if we don't publish skyjackings, all sorts of rumors will float around, people won't know what they should know about a matter of some importance to air travelers and airlines and investors—and the general public, in fact. But I read where the airport traffic controllers called for a blackout on coverage of skyjackings suggesting that such stories provide an incentive for more skyjacks."

"I, for one, am getting damn upset with suggestions that we shouldn't publish this or that. One guy says we shouldn't print some foreign policy news because it might damage the national interest, another guy does not want to embarrass the government, he does not want embarrassing news printed, a third guy does not want us to print anything that might hurt business here in town, somebody else says crime news and news of demonstrations makes for more of those—pretty soon we won't be able to print anything but the weather report and I suppose some clown will complain that we jinx the weather and make it bad when the weather man predicts it would be good." Burt said it loudly.

Charlene had a milder comment. "I agree with all that, Burt, but I think we could be a little careful with details on how skyjacks and other crimes are done, particularly when we cover terrorists. The public does not need to know all the fine details."

"You are talking about suppression, and furthermore, the public wants to know those details and they have a right to know them," Burt said.

"Even if it means more crime?" Charlene asked. "I remember hearing of a story we did such a detailed job on that some guys knew the bank had been robbed because the guard was on his coffee break at 2, and so they came back a day later and robbed it at 2."

"The bank should have changed the guard's coffee break after the first stick-up. That's not our fault," Burt said. "Besides if you are going to push this argument, we're going to be covering up a lot of important stuff and who knows where it will stop."

"Well, if you had a story that would serve no purpose except to embarrass the family of a criminal, wouldn't you suppress it in the public good? What if it would ruin the town?" Charlene was enjoying the argument.

"I can't think of any stories like that and if I could I'd print them," Burt said.

"What if it meant the newspaper would go out of business?"

Burt slammed down his fist. "Be realistic and come down to earth."

Questions for discussion

1. Do stories of airline skyjackings contribute to additional skyjackings? How about details in these and other crime stories?

2. Can you think of any stories of the type Charlene suggests might be suppressed? Would you suppress them? Why or why not?

3. At what point in the details of crime does the public's right to know stop. The need to know? The desire to know?

CHAPTER XXVI
THE MURDER

I t's three espressos time again," Charlene said. "God, covering that murder story was distasteful."

"I thought it was a pretty good story," Burt commented. "You got a quote from the victim's widow, there was plenty of gore in it, we had a sharp photo of the corpse in a litter-strewn apartment and I bet we sold 2,000 more newspapers on the street."

"That's what's bothering me. I didn't want to talk to the widow; she was in near hysterics, but I did manage to get a quote about her husband's recent whereabouts. You should have heard the jackass from the TV station ask if she would miss her husband and how she would feel knowing he had been murdered. That brought on renewed hysterics, all of which were duly recorded by the camera. We sure have been down on the TV news folks lately.

"As for all those details about the crushed skull and blood on the floor, that was the desk's idea. I also think they socked it to the suspect pretty hard, damn near convicted him with circumstantial evidence," Charlene said.

"Yeah," Mark said, "I thought we were supposed to be careful with that stuff. Can he get a fair trial? Some prosecutors have lost convictions due to that kind of pre-trial publicity—maybe it does prejudice a ,jury. The defense is sure to ask for a change of venue."

"I don't think we went so far as to break the rules—which are an in-fringement on press freedom, anyway," Burt said. "After all, the guy was arrested and the evidence does not look good.

"You should have seen how we would have played that in Chicago in the old days," Burt said. "We would have gotten six pictures of the guy if we had to steal them. He's been arrested and it's news, man.

" People have a right to know who has been arrested and how the evidence stacks up against him. He's going to be tried by public opinion, anyway. What the cops do is important to the public. The public needs to know it," Burt said.

"Well, I think we invaded that widow's privacy. It's bad enough calling people for obits; I'd much rather talk to the mortuary, though some people seem to like to spill it out." Charlene said

"Legally, we didn't invade her privacy; she was a newsworthy figure. Movie stars and many people in the public eye or the news—whether they want to be or not—give up some privacy," Mark said.

"Your question," he concluded, "is whether we ethically should have."

Questions for discussion

1. Identify the several ethical issues raised in the above. Comment on each.

2. In the larger sense, and in several contexts, discuss the public's right to know and the public's need to know.

CHAPTER XXVII
THE NEXT DAY

The charges against that guy they had in the murder yesterday are going to be dropped. Turns out he's alibied real good. I just got through writing a story getting him off the hook. And, thank God, the lawyers say we didn't libel him—not that he's likely to sue, though we must have skated pretty close." Charlene looked relieved.

"Well, I hope the second story is prominent," Mark said. "It disturbs me when we run the dismissal stories back in the paper.

"Along those lines, it also bothers me whenever we have a big story and just let it drop," he added.

"Some readers just have to wonder what has happened.," Burt said. "But that's because more important news has come along, we're involved in other more timely stories, or the public has lost interest, It's not really intentional."

Questions for discussion

1. Can you find examples of a "dismissal" story running back inside the newspaper or not running at all after a page one arrest story? Why does such coverage occur?

2. Can you find examples of stories that are just allowed to die? Why does this occur?

3. Can you find examples where neither of the above have been allowed to occur?

CHAPTER XXVIII
THE MASQUERADE

Turned down a big assignment today, probably cost me a raise," Mark said, to open the evening's coffee klatch activities and talkfest.

"Another great foreign correspondent lost," Burt said sarcastically.

"Not really.," Mark replied. "They wanted me to assume a false identity to do a big expose. It looked like a sure way to get into real legal trouble for no good reason because we can get the story without the masquerade.

"The story," Mark continued, "is about lack of discipline in the schools, particularly that the high school students are pushing and shoving each other in the halls and writing 'vulgar and obscene' graffiti on the walls and the teachers aren't doing a thing about it. They wanted me to go to the high schools, adopt a pose for being there—a big brother of a student, a parent, anything but a reporter or interested citizen—and hang around a few days."

Burt said, "I've seen cases where adopting a false identity or engaging in some kind of stunt turns up a mighty readable piece and often a good expose. You know, reporter goes to jail, reporter goes to hospital, reporter tries to get welfare—all disguised."

"Wouldn't take much of a disguise to get welfare," Charlene interjected. "All I'd have to do is show them my paycheck."

Mark wanted to return to the case at hand. "There are state laws about unauthorized people hanging around schools and I don't think I want to test whether they violate the first amendment. Besides, I know the guys at the high school. They'll let me walk around there any time I want to without advance notice if I just stop by the principal's office and tell him I'm there. And I know a bunch of students and teachers who would be good sources. I think the editor is just looking to win a contest and he thinks these masquerades impress the judges."

Questions for discussion

1. Under what circumstances should journalists engage in stunts and masquerades? Can you find or think of any cases (some are quite famous) where they have resulted in major stories?

2. Would you have accepted the assignment Burt turned down? Why or why not?

3. What do you think about masquerades in the reverse direction, i.e., police masquerading as reporters?

CHAPTER XXIX
THE THUNDERING HERD

Man, you look beat and all dragged out," Burt observed as Charlene approached the regular table in the coffeehouse. "We almost had a riot at the airport—I got shoved around and knocked down," Charlene said. "I should have knocked somebody's teeth down his throat."

"The customers getting rough?" Mark asked.

"Not the customers, the distinguished representatives of the news media. That congressman whose wife and kids were just killed this morning in a plane crash in the east came through. He'd scheduled a brief stopover and press conference. Thought it might draw two or three reporters while he was between planes. As soon as the news of his family got out, there must have been 50 guys there to greet him. He'd tried to cancel the press conference and stay in seclusion. But there was no way. When he came off that plane, the reporters brushed right past the fuzz and roared around, screaming and hollering, shoving each other out of the way and that's when I got knocked down. They shoved microphones and cameras in his face."

"Damn, that's worse than coverage by the herd; that's gross," Mark said. "I really think we need to arrange for pool reporters in cases like that. You know, select a few guys, from the wire services probably, and let them relay the stuff. A crowd of reporters can mess things up even if they don't get as bad as your crowd today."

"Trouble with that is everybody wants to be on the spot. To make sure they get it right and for the prestige of being on the scene." Burt obviously wasn't going to jump in any pools. "What if they'd selected some illiterate cub from the Toonerville Times?"

<u>Questions for discussion</u>

1. Explore the advantages and disadvantages of pool reporting?
2. Do you know of any cases where "coverage by the herd" has been harmful? What alternatives can you suggest?

CHAPTER XXX
A SACRED COW MOOS

I'm in trouble with the desk again," Charlene said. "I slammed one of the local businessmen pretty good today by reporting that he was in some deep trouble with the criminal law several years ago. I wrapped it into an account of his arrest last night for punching a guy in a night club. Turns out he's one of the publisher's best friends. The copyeditor said the publisher didn't want the story killed, but did we have to go to work on the guy's past?"

Burt said, "I saw your story, and I know the guy you mean. H e l l , everyone knows he's a sacred cow."

"Well, I wish they'd print lists of sacred cows. Besides, there shouldn't be any sacred cows," Charlene said. "All the local charities and the publisher's clubs would be on it.

"The trouble is, we don't really know if there are. Some reporters and editors think somebody's a sacred cow but it's just folklore. The publisher does not think so; it's just some story that goes back years."

"I've heard of papers that do have sacred cow lists and lists of taboos too," Burt said. "Things you can't print. But that's largely a thing of the past and we really don't have any—your story ran."

"Some taboos are that way too," Burt said. "I always thought we couldn't, under any circumstances, print an article favorable to gambling. But there was no rule against it and we do it all the time. Of course, there are some common sense taboos like don't print needlessly gory pictures."

"Well, I think taboo subjects and words—like sacred cows—ought to be written down and passed out in the city room. No, really I think we shouldn't have either," Charlene said.

"We have a pamphlet of editorial guidelines, and it says, for example, that we will not poke fun at religions or at people in trouble or the handicapped. You might call that a taboo, but I'd say it is just good common sense," Mark said.

Questions for discussion:

1. Can you think of some taboos? Some sacred cows on your local newspaper?

2. What should properly be taboo? Should anyone be a sacred cow?

3. Should taboos be written down? Should lists of persons considered for special treatment be written down?

4. Should there be ANY taboos or ANYONE singled out for favorable or unfavorable treatment? Should newspapers have guidelines such as the one Mark mentions?

5. What deeper ethical issues do the above questions raise?

CHAPTER XXXI
THE HOAX

I saw a story on the wire today about a guy who claimed his dog had given birth to cats. Claimed he had proof. That story comes up every 10 years or so, and it's a fake. I threw it away. Experience pays."

Burt made that statement, but he wasn't laughing. "I've been taken in before by hoaxes, frauds and fakes, and I think everyone in the business should be more careful. It is embarrassing as hell when it turns out we've been done in, and it's happened to some mighty important newspapers and wire services in the past."

"On local stories, it's largely a matter of checking and rechecking," Mark said. "I don't think we do enough of that anyway. We take people's word for what happened—the police, for example—without really checking.

"Trouble is, it takes time and sometimes there are things you just can't check."

Questions for discussion

1. Can you find any frauds or hoaxes that have fooled newspapers and the public in the past? How could these have been prevented?

2. To what extent should a newsman or a desk go to check a story?

CHAPTER XXXII
THE BEARD

Some of my friends are getting so teed off at our newspaper that they are going to start an alternate sheet, I swear," Charlene said. "That will provide some competition and a lot of hippie stores will advertise in it and a lot of young people will stop reading our paper and read theirs."

"What's got them so fired up?" Mark asked.

"They are mad about the way we described and identified the three guys picked up yesterday for demonstrating at the school office," Charlene said. "We identified them as 'long-haired, bearded hippie-types'."

"That's because that's the way the cops described them," Burt said. "That ID is just as important as their ages and addresses."

"And a lot of people are angry with the cops for hippie-stereotyping," Mark said. "You know, they see the old car, the dog, the odd clothes and the beads, and they make a traffic stop.."

"Someone needs to talk to the cops," he added.

"It's stereotyped and provides nothing. We don't describe a business-man who is arrested as a clean-shaven, short-haired country club type, do we?" said Charlene.

"Pertinent identification—that's what we need and that's why we don't use racial identifications unless they are pertinent," Mark said. "This hippie stuff sounds like something from the last century."

"Well, a lot of people think 'hippie-type' means something, and it's part of the news," Burt said. "We have to supply appropriate identification for people who make news. I don't see any way out."

Questions for discussion

1. Is there a "way out"? Should there be?

2. What identification is pertinent? Are some kinds of identification pertinent in some circumstances and not others?

3. Is "hippie-stereotyping" a police problem? A media problem? Both?

CHAPTER XXXIII
THE PLAGIARIST

I see by the wires that another hot shot East Coast reporter got fired today for plagiarism. Now how many does that Make?" Mark asked to open the conversation.

"Too many," Burt replied. "How these guys think they can get away with it, I'm sure I don't know."

"I t used to be that it was columnists that got caught, now it seems to be the reporters," Charlene said. "It has to be a firing offense anywhere."

"I think columnists have a big problem coming up with new ideas day after day," Mark said. "Then they panic when they are staring at their keyboards on deadline and so they grab a column that's on the web or in some far-off newspaper.

"Sometimes reporters say they have information in their notes and they forgot where they got it, but with columnists it has be intentional if they grab whole sections."

"It will sure get you fired here, whether you are a reporter or a columnist, and so will making up quotes or faking it in any other way," Burt said.

"It isn't just journalists who have to worry about plagiarism," Charlene said. "Academics, book writers, playwrights, poets and song writers should all be concerned.

"And journalists don't use footnotes or bibliographies in our pieces like academics do," she added.

Mark said, "It is not just an ethical problem, it is an important legal issue—my media law professor says she is devoting more and more time to intellectual property rights. And the new electronic technology—the web and so forth—has made matters even more complicated."

"They say there are gray areas in plagiarism but it seems to me that if you are using someone else's stuff, you need to get permission and give credit," Charlene said.

"You'd think that with all the firings for piracy, people would stop plagiarizing but then there's another example like today," Burt said. "These guys ought to fly a skull and crossbones."

Questions for discussion:

1. Is there a " gray area" in incorporating the work of others into your story? What is it?

2. Is the use of other people's work in your piece ever justified? Under what circumstances?

3. What are some other reasons why people plagiarize?
4.

CHAPTER XXXIV
THE CIVIC JOURNALIST

My mass comm. seminar was talking about a movement in the news media called Civic Journalism," Mark said. "Sounds pretty interesting."

"You are behind the times," Burt said. "That was hot in the 19 90s when a big foundation was pushing it with conventions, videos, and sponsorship."

"What is it?" Charlene wanted to know.

"It means that journalists should get back in touch with their communities," Mark said. "News organizations should sponsor town meetings, get reporters out in the neighborhoods, try to identify local problems and seek solutions

"The professor even had examples of where, in one case, a newspaper didn't just report on crime—they went out into high crime areas and tried to root out the basic problem and find solutions.," he added.

"Well, I don't like it," Burt said. "You are getting involved in the story. In the old days we were told to stay out of the story and just be objective observers."

"But newspapers have always sponsored charity 10K races, spelling bees, and summer camp funds so how is this different?" Charlene wanted to know.

"What if a newspaper or broadcast station sponsored a community meeting on, say, the homeless, and it turned into a near riot with angry insults hurled on both sides of the issue," Burt said. "Wouldn't there be a lot of pressure to put the best face on it? It's our meeting."

"Circulation isn't exactly soaring," Mark said. "Maybe newspapers and broadcast stations need to reconnect with their communities and get more involved in identifying problems and seeking solutions," Mark said.

Charlene said, "There's been a lot of talk in the news biz about rebuilding trust and credibility with our audiences. Maybe Civic Journalism is one way to do it..

"There's an old saying in newsrooms," Burt said. " you can't be the drama critic if you are director of the community theater."

Questions for discussion:

1. . What is the current status of the Civic Journalism movement? Do you know of any examples of Civic Journalism?

2. Civic Journalism (sometimes called Public Journalism) seems to suggest a new role for the media. Is it now time for journalists to redefine their role?

3. Would you like to be a Civic Journalist? Why or why not?

CHAPTER XXXV
THE SOURCE

I've got a good source at City Hall and he says the Mayor is using his office expense fund for campaign advertising," Charlene said.

"Trouble us, the source won't go on the record and he may have some proof but I have to swear that I will never reveal my source's identity to anyone. How firm is our policy that an editor has to know your source?"

"You are not going to be able to do that," Mark said. "The Managing Editor has an 'absolutely no exceptions' policy that if you grant your course anonymity , you have to tell your editor who your source is. That hasn't come up for awhile."

Charlene said, "What if my source won't let me do that?"

"Then you better find another source because there are no exceptions to that rule," Mark said. "The problem is there have been too many outrageous examples of reporters making up stories and then saying they got it from a source they can't identify to anyone. Remember this came up when you did another big story." (see chapter 17)

Besides, we are always talking about credibility and trust with our readers and anonymous sources don't build either," Mark added.

"OK, what if I get him to agree to telling my editor who he is, what about the court appearance?" Charlene wanted to know. "What if this winds up in court and I have to testify? I couldn't break my promise to my source. How good is our shield law?"

Mark said, "In this state and many others, you are probably OK because we have a shield law that protects reporters from having to reveal a source in court. But you can't count on the judge not finding some loophole, and if the judge finds you in contempt of court for not testifying, you could wind up in jail."

"No way," Charlene said. "The First Amendment should protect reporters from having to reveal their sources. Lots of great investigative stories were based on secret sources."

"Well, the courts have ruled that the First Amendment doesn't do that and there is no federal shield law," so you better think twice," Mark said.

Burt said, " I know some reporters who won't take info from a source they can't identify and some reporters won't take off-the-record stuff either."

"Can't you find a source who will go on the record and be identified," Mark asked.

"I guess I may have to," Charlene said.

Questions for discussion:

1. What would you do if you were Charlene?

2. Should there be a federal shield law? Should the courts interpret the Constitution as the right to keep their sources secret under the First Amendment?

CHAPTER XXXVI
THE MEDIA MERGER

I hear we are all going to be TV stars," Charlene said. "The bosses are going to merge the newsroom and we will go on TV and radio or write for our website as well as our newspaper."

"It's all the rage in journalism education," Mark said. "The trend is called media convergence and now students are supposed to learn how to report for various media, or platforms, as the professor calls them.

"The broadcast facilities are going to be in our newsroom, and you are going to write for TV and radio and the web as our newspaper and extra copies of the same story won't cut it—you have do a different story for each one," he added.

"I think we should get paid more if we are going to have our stuff used on different media," Charlene said. "I hope no broadcast journalists lose their jobs in this merger. Besides, I don't want go on TV—you have to put on a lot of makeup and they want you to wear an ugly blazer."

Burt said, " When I broke into this business, I heard that in the 70s, when newsrooms were going electronic, some reporters said they wouldn't write on computers. And you know what the suits told them? My way or the highway."

Mark said, "I think the real problem is that writing for radio or appearing on TV is very different from writing for print. You really do have to learn new techniques. The J school is having problems with merged media courses."

"I wasn't happy when they started putting our stories on the newspaper's website without paying us extra," Charlene said. "And remember how that was going to be a cash cow?"

"That cow has been very quiet lately," Burt said. "I remember when we used to compete with the broadcast journalists. Now we are supposed to be working together."

Charlene said, " One editor told me that I might be able to expand on my story and even tell how I sourced it when I go on TV. I don't think that's possible, TV newscasts are so tight that two minutes is in eternity."

Burt said, "I tried out for a TV news job once and the editor told me I had a great face for radio. Now I'm going to be on TV. All you have to do is read the Teleprompter and look cute, right?"

"It is harder than that, you have to deal with moving images," Mark said. "But don't worry, training seminars start Monday."

Questions for discussion:

1. Does merging newsrooms reduce competition or is it in the public interest?

2. Should reporters be paid more money when newsrooms are merged?

INDEX OF ISSUES
(References are to CHAPTER numbers, not pages)

SUGGESTIONS FOR BACKGROUND &
ADDITIONAL READING

Periodicals: Columbia Journalism Review (Columbia University Graduate School of Journalism), Nieman Reports (Nieman Foundation at Harvard University), Quill (Society of Professional Journalists), and American Journalism Review (College of Journalism, University of Maryland) are excellent sources for current controversies in news media ethics. Publications such as the trade journals Editor & Publisher and Broadcasting and Cable sometimes treat ethical issues. The American Editor (American Society of Newspaper Editors) and the online Associated Press Managing Editors Association's APME Update (www.apme.com/updates) and similar online sites for newspapers and broadcasting often report on issues of interest. The Journal of Mass Media Ethics (Erlbaum) provides more philosophical discussions and Media Ethics (Emerson College), the magazine serving mass communication ethics, publishes in-depth commentary. The publications, programs and online information available from the Poynter Institute of St. Petersburg, Florida, are renowned for their contribution to responsible and quality journalism (www.poynter.com)

Books: A large number of general works deal with mass communications, the role of mass communications in society, and press responsibility. One of the best of the classic works is Responsibility in Mass Communication (New York: Harper & Row, 1969) by William L. Rivers and Wilbur Schramm. A seminal work by the Commission of Freedom of the Press, A Free and Responsible Press (Chicago: U, of Chicago Press, 1947), presents the social responsibility theorists' views. Dr. Robert M. Hutchins headed the commission. Important recent works include Media Ethics: Cases and Moral Reasoning by Clifford Christians, Kim B. Rotzoll, Mark Fowler, and Kathy Brittain McKee (New York: Addison Wesley Longman, 2001, sixth edition), Deni Elliott (ed.) Responsible Journalism Beverly Hills, CA, Sage 1986; Edward

B. Lambeth's <u>Committed Journalism: An Ethic for the Profession</u> (Bloomington, Indiana University Press, 1986, and Philip Meyer's <u>Ethical Journalism: A Guide for Students, Practitioners, and Consumers</u> (White Plains: Longman, 1987); and many works by John C. Merrill and his various co-authors. Particularly interesting is his <u>Legacy of Wisdom: Great Thinkers and Journalism</u> (Ames: Iowa State University Press, 1994). Ben H. Bagdikian, a regular commentator on the press, is the author of important works on media ownership, especially <u>The Media Monopoly</u> (Boston: Beacon, 1997, fifth edition). Now outdated, but still interesting, are works by the late A.J. Leibling, the New Yorker critic, including <u>The Wayward Pressman</u> (New York: Doubleday, 1948) and <u>The Press</u> (New York: Ballantine, 1964).

In terms of my use of texts, I have found Conrad C. Fink's <u>Media Ethics</u> (Needham Heights, MA: Allyn and Bacon, 1995) and Louis Alva Day's <u>Ethics in Media Communications: Cases and Controversies</u> (Belmont, CA: Wadsworth/Thompson Learning, 2002, fourth edition) especially valuable.

The Association for Education in Journalism and Mass Communication Education publications <u>Journalism and Mass Communications Educator</u> and <u>Journalism and Mass Communications Quarterly</u> can help students and teachers keep abreast of new works. <u>Journalism and Mass Communication Quarterly</u> publishes significant research in mass communication.